CUSTOMER SERVICE
TIP OF THE WEEK

CUSTOMER SERVICE
TIP OF THE WEEK

Over 52 ideas and reminders
to sharpen your skills

JEFF TOISTER

Cover and Interior Design:

Anne C. Kerns, Anne Likes Red, Inc.

TABLE OF CONTENTS

ACKNOWLEDGEMENTS vii

INTRODUCTION 1

CHAPTER ONE: How to Use This Book 7

CHAPTER TWO: The Thank You Letter Challenge 17

CHAPTER THREE: Build Rapport 27

CHAPTER FOUR: Exceed Expectations 67

CHAPTER FIVE: Solve Problems 107

CHAPTER SIX: Resources for Customer Service Leaders . . . 147

ACKNOWLEDGEMENTS

This book is dedicated to all the customer service professionals who work hard every day to serve customers.

I admire you for your dedication, your concern for others, and your genuine desire to make someone else's day better.

INTRODUCTION

"The great thing I have found with your weekly customer service tips is that everyone has a chance to take or apply the tip in a different way, in their own way."

—**Denie,** *Area Customer Experience Manager*

The **Customer Service Tip of the Week** started out like many business ideas: it came out of trying to solve a problem for a customer.

I was meeting with Sue Thompson, who at the time ran the transportation and parking department at Oregon Health and Science University (OHSU). She had hired me to facilitate customer service training for her team, and they had worked hard to develop a reputation at OHSU for outstanding service. Now Thompson was concerned about sustaining her team's progress.

She knew that people could slide back into old habits without constant reinforcement, so she and her management team regularly discussed service in team meetings and one-on-one conversations. At the same time, Thompson felt it would be helpful to have a reinforcement message that came from someone besides herself or her management team.

I suggested a simple reminder system, and offered to set up an automated email list that her employees could subscribe to. Each email would contain a single customer service tip related to something we had talked about in training. The emails would be sent once per week to provide regular reminders while giving employees time to try out each tip with their customers.

Thompson agreed to the suggestion and we implemented the weekly emails with great success. "We often discussed the tips during our weekly staff meeting," she said. "It really got the ball rolling on people sharing their experiences and ideas for consistently working on and improving our service. These improvements were quantified in our drastically improved customer service scores and in the many unsolicited accolades all areas of the department received from our customers."

Over time, Thompson found the weekly tips helped her team stay focused on service. "Working in parking, the team was reminded regularly that the only thing we sold was customer service, so we had to be the absolute best at it. The weekly tips reminded us of this and that it was up to us to create that culture of exceptional customer service."

I quickly decided to make the weekly emails available to anyone who wanted to subscribe to them. Today, thousands of customer service professionals all over the world receive the *Customer Service Tip of the Week* email each Monday.

This book is the next step in the evolution. Many subscribers have asked me for a way to put all the tips in one place. The *Customer Service Tip of the Week* is that resource.

Who Should Use This Book?

The book is intended to be a resource for both frontline customer service professionals and customer service leaders. It's designed to be applicable to any customer service environment or industry.

If you're relatively new to customer service, you'll find proven tips and ideas to help you quickly develop your skills. Don't be afraid to experiment with different techniques to see which ones work best for you.

Some of the tips will be familiar to experienced service professionals. Consider these as helpful reminders. There are many skills and techniques we know we should use but, over time, can get out of the habit of using.

Customer service leaders will also find plenty of helpful tools for sharing the tips with their teams. If you lead or train customer service employees, Chapter Six was created especially for you. The suggestions and activities it contains have all been tested by customer service leaders who have used the tips to help keep their teams focused on outstanding service.

Why Weekly Reminders Are Helpful

Adults learn and retain information through repetition and novelty.

Repetition is important, because we need to access knowledge multiple times before it really sticks. You're much more likely to remember a tip when you read it in an email, discuss it with a colleague, and practice it with a customer (versus just reading it once).

Novelty is also important, because we quickly grow tired of hearing the same message repeated the same way, over and over again. That's why the tip changes each week. There's a new weekly tip for just over a year before the tips reset and the first one comes out again.

I chose the weekly cadence (versus some other time frame) because it fits a natural workflow. Many of us start each week by reviewing our plans, projects, and challenges. We then move forward to accomplish as much as possible before taking a couple of well-earned weekend days off and then starting all over again. Sharing one tip per week fits that natural flow.

Get the Tips Via Email

The *Customer Service Tip of the Week* email is still going strong. You can subscribe for free to get one tip via email, once per week. The emails also include links to blog posts, videos, and other resources you can use to gain additional knowledge and insight about that week's tip.

Here's the link: **toistersolutions.com/tips**

Notes

There are plenty of empty spaces throughout the book like the one below. You can use them to take notes.

CHAPTER ONE: HOW TO USE THIS BOOK

"I love getting the Customer Service Tip of the Week *in my inbox. It's a great jumping-off point for our weekly team meeting. I present it to the team for consideration, and rather than me just deciding to make changes, we discuss and the whole team has input. It helps me get greater buy-in from them and helps them feel empowered enough to make impactful changes."*

—Lance Hendrickson, *Head of Support, CoSchedule*

The *Customer Service Tip of the Week* tips are designed to augment more formal customer service training. Training classes are great, but we tend to forget what we learn soon after the class if we don't reinforce it! And in some organizations, employees don't have the opportunity to attend formal training, yet they still want to develop their skills.

That's where these tips come in.

The weekly tips started out as a free email service (it still is: **toistersolutions.com/tips**). But when you receive the tips via email, it's the tip I've selected. Sometimes that's exactly what you need. Other times, the tip is just a nice reminder of something you're already doing well.

This book puts more than 52 tips all in one place so you can pick and choose which tips you'd like to focus on. The book assumes you'll do this on a weekly schedule, but of course you're free to choose whatever time frame you'd prefer, whether that's daily, weekly, or even monthly.

How to Use the Tips

Customer service is very much in the moment. It's difficult to pause and turn to a list of ideas when you're in the middle of serving someone. We tend to operate on instinct, doing the best we can to serve our customers.

The opportunity to change our approach happens before and after an interaction.

We can set an intention to act a certain way before serving a customer. The intention helps us choose our actions. Afterwards, we can reflect on what went well and what we want to improve.

These customer service tips will help guide your intentions and reflections.

Here are five steps you can take to use these tips to enhance your customer service skills. (If you're a customer service leader, you can follow these steps to help develop your team.)

STEP ONE: Select a Tip.
Later in this chapter, you'll find several strategies for selecting a specific tip to focus on. Chapter Six gives customer service leaders additional ideas for selecting tips to share with their teams.

STEP TWO: Reflect on the Tip.
Read the tip and think about whether you've used it in the past. If you did, what went well and not so well? If you haven't used it yet, try to think back to situations where it could have been useful. For instance, tip number six (see Chapter Three) is to learn and use customer names. You might think about situations when you've called a customer by name in the past, and reflect on how using their name helped build rapport. You could also think about challenges you've faced, such as when a customer's name is difficult to pronounce.

STEP THREE: Create an Intention.

What specific ways can you apply the tip in your daily work? For example, if you were working on using customer names, you might think of some different ways you could learn your customer's name and use it in conversation.

STEP FOUR: Practice the Tip.

This is when you use the tip while serving customers. The *Customer Service Tip of the Week* approach gives you a week to practice the tip, so you become really good at using it and start building a new habit. For instance, if you were trying to use customer names, you might notice that you're much more comfortable and proficient at the end of the week than you were at the beginning of the week.

STEP FIVE: Evaluate Your Progress.

You can review how things are going throughout the week and make adjustments as you go. It's also helpful to take a moment at the end of the week and think about how you used the tip. Try to remember what went well and what, if anything, you found challenging. Think about how using the tip affected the way you interacted with customers and how you can continue using the tip in the future.

Following the five steps each week will help you build a strong set of customer service skills. You'll create better relationships with customers, discover how you can meet or exceed their expectations, and solve problems more effectively.

How to Select a Tip

There are many different ways to select the tips you want to focus on. If you're a customer service leader or trainer, I've written Chapter Six just for you. That chapter contains exercises for you to do with your team to identify a schedule of tips to share, discuss, and try. In the meantime, here are three options for selecting tips that will be relevant to you and your team.

TIPS BY CATEGORY

One option is to select tips by category. My research shows that there are three basic skill categories for customer service: building relationships, exceeding expectations, and solving problems. Chapters Three, Four, and Five are organized around those skills:

- Chapter Three: *Building Relationships*

- Chapter Four: *Exceeding Expectations*

- Chapter Five: *Solving Problems*

Start by selecting one of these categories to focus on. Then work your way through each chapter, focusing on one tip per week. Or you can pick and choose the tips you think are most relevant and useful to you.

11

TIPS BY CHALLENGE

Another option is to select tips by the specific issue or challenge you are trying to solve.

Customer Service Tip of the Week email subscribers often email me to share a particular challenge they're working on. I reviewed hundreds of emails to see what challenges are shared most often.

Here are the top ten customer service challenges people have shared with me. I've included four tips that can help with each one, so you can pick one challenge to focus on for a month and use a new tip each week during that time.

Challenge	Recommended Tips
Service culture, whether it's creating one or being part of one	1. The Thank You Letter Challenge 10. Use "We," Not "They" 29. Use the Platinum Rule 33. Do an After-Action Review
New job or new role within the company	2. Be You 6. Learn and Use Customer Names 7. Make Sure Customers Know Your Name 18. Focus on Lifetime Value
Delivering memorable "wow" experiences	14. Give Preferential Treatment 19. Customers Determine the Extra Mile 30. Treat Everyone Like a VIP 32. Add Some Extra Shine
Serving difficult or upset customers	44. Acknowledge and Refocus 45. Avoid Trigger Words 46. Avoid Quoting Policy 49. The Good Cop, Bad Cop Technique

Challenge	Recommended Tips
Using customer feedback to improve service	12. Build an Interest List 25. Avoid Assumptions 50. Share Customer Feedback 51. Beware of Icebergs
Staying motivated	17. Take a Break and Recharge 22. Cut Afternoon Caffeine 37. Stop Complaining 52. Anchor Your Attitude
Recovering from service failures	38. Empathize with Customers 39. Take It Personally 47. Overcorrect Problems 48. The Partner Technique
Handling tricky or difficult problems	36. Expand Your Influence 41. Bend the Rules 42. Be the Point Person 43. The Pre-Emptive Acknowledgement
Breaking the ice with customers	4. Make the First Move 13. Find Something in Common 15. Answer the Phone with Enthusiasm 16. Use the 10 and 5 Rule
Improving listening skills	3. Serve One Customer at a Time 8. The Five Question Technique 23. Paraphrase to Confirm Understanding 27. Listen for Emotional Needs
Bonus: Serving customers via email	9. Check Your Email Before Sending It 21. Avoid Multitasking 24. Slow Down When Reading Email 26. Anticipate the Next Question

START WITH TIP #1

The third option is to simply work through the tips in sequential order: 1–53, plus a few bonus tips. There's enough here to take you through an entire year before you start all over again.

I've included 53 tips because I expect many readers will start with a new tip each Monday. The *Customer Service Tip of the Week* emails are sent out each Monday, unless it's a U.S. holiday, in which case the email goes out on a Tuesday. There are 52 Mondays some years, while other years have 53.

Remember that these tips are designed to help you build and maintain your skills, so repeating tips is a good thing. We all need a refresher from time to time.

I've put my most important tip at number one with this in mind. It's a powerful exercise that guides you through the process of creating your personal customer service vision. You'll find a complete description in Chapter Two.

Let's Connect!

When people sign up for my *Customer Service Tip of the Week* email, they receive an automated message confirming their subscription. The message also invites subscribers to reply and send me a personal email to let me know what they're working on. I often have terrific conversations with subscribers and will frequently suggest additional resources or tips that might be helpful.

I invite you to do the same. You'll find my personal contact information below. Please drop me a line and let me know what you're working on in customer service. It could be a new initiative, a specific challenge, or a success story you achieved from using one of these tips!

EMAIL: jeff@toistersolutions.com

CALL/TEXT: 619-955-7946

CHAPTER TWO:
THE THANK YOU LETTER CHALLENGE

"Here's what happened in my Thank You Letter Challenge: I did receive a thank you, verbally, that was almost verbatim to what I had written down. The letter kept my attitude in the right spot and reminded me of the level of customer service I choose to deliver each and every day. It essentially became my mission statement."

—Terry, *Customer Service Manager*

People often ask me if I could share just one customer service tip, what would it be?

THE ANSWER IS TO HAVE A VISION.

This involves thinking about the quality of service you'd like to provide, **from your customer's perspective.**

Let's say you work in technical support, helping people solve issues with their computer software. You might create a vision that focuses on how your customers experience relief when a frustrating problem is finally resolved. Having that ultimate goal, helping your customer experience relief, makes it easier to figure out the right thing to do in almost every situation.

NOTES

TIP #1

The Thank You Letter Challenge

A fun way to create this vision is through an activity called the Thank You Letter Challenge. Here's how it works:

1. Write a thank you letter that you'd hope to receive from a customer.

2. Read the letter each day for 21 days.

3. Try to receive a real version of the letter from an actual customer.

I know it can be difficult to stick to a program, even for just 21 days, so I've created a daily reminder email to help you. Each reminder prompts you to read your letter, and also gives you a tip for turning that letter into reality.

YOU CAN SIGN UP FOR THE REMINDERS HERE:
toistersolutions.com/thankyou

Thank You Letter Example

I like to revisit this activity myself once a year. Here's the thank you letter I wrote on January 19, 2017:

. . . .

Dear Jeff,

Thank you for helping me lead my customer service team to new heights. Our customers are happier and employees are more committed than ever before.

—A. Client

. . . .

The letter is very short and simple. It also reflects my company's mission, *Help customer service teams unlock their hidden potential.*

Starting on January 19th, I read this letter at the beginning of every day for 21 days. It made me think about how I interacted with clients and potential clients. My goal during every interaction was to help that person lead their customer service team to better results.

Two weeks later, I received an email from Erin, a customer service manager who was asking for help. She wanted to know how to manage an employee with a bad attitude. Erin explained how one or two employees were negatively influencing the rest of the team; she was trying to find a way to turn things around.

Keeping my thank you letter in mind, I wrote her a detailed response explaining what I had done in a similar situation. I had learned from experience that it's more productive to focus on specific, observable behaviors and avoid mentioning subjective judgments (such as the employee having a bad attitude). I had tried to talk to an employee about a bad attitude myself once, and it did not go well. The conversation went much better when I focused on specific behaviors instead.

A day later, Erin wrote back to me:

....

Hi Jeff,

Thank you again. You really do lead by example, and go the extra mile. I really appreciate your help.

I had a meeting with one of the agents today and overall it went well. I did not reference anything about a bad attitude, but focused more on the behaviors themselves and she couldn't argue with it. She understood where I was coming from and said she would work on changing her approach.

We'll see how things go in the next week. Thank you again. I really appreciate you taking the time to follow up.

Take care.

Erin, Customer Service Manager

....

Wow! I was so happy for Erin. And her detailed letter was very close to the thank you letter I had written. The exercise was a success!

By the way, I posted this advice on LinkedIn, and it quickly become one of my most popular articles with over 60,000 people reading it! You can read it here: **https://www.linkedin. com/pulse/how-manage-employee-bad-attitude-jeff- toister-cplp-phr/**

Bonus Information

Think about the companies best known for customer service. There are probably a few that immediately come to mind. I wrote a book called *The Service Culture Handbook,* in which I studied what makes these companies special; it provides a step-by-step formula that other companies can follow.

The number one trait of customer-focused companies is a customer service vision. I describe this as a shared definition of outstanding customer service that gets everyone on the same page. Here are a few examples:

Publix was named the #1 retailer in the United States for 2017 by the American Customer Satisfaction Index. It's a chain of grocery stores primarily located in the southeastern part of the country. Publix's customer service vision is, *"Where shopping is a pleasure."* The entire company is focused on making shopping a more pleasurable experience for its customers.

JetBlue Airways was the highest-rated airline on the American Customer Satisfaction Index in 2017. It's rated even higher than the legendary Southwest Airlines! JetBlue's customer service vision is, *"Inspire humanity."* The company is focused on bringing a more human touch to air travel in an era when many of its competitors have experienced well-publicized incidents of poor passenger treatment.

Does your company have a customer service vision? Sometimes a company doesn't have one, but an individual team or department within the organization does.

I recommend referencing your company's or team's customer service vision when you write your thank you letter, since your personal vision should be consistent with the bigger picture.

If your company, department, or team doesn't have a customer service vision, you can use the thank you letter exercise to help shape your own customer service philosophy. Think about the type of service you're bringing to your customers on those days when everything just seems to work right.

And then remember to read
your thank you letter every
day for the next 21 days.

It's an amazingly uplifting experience to write your thank you letter and see it become reality!

CHAPTER THREE: BUILD RAPPORT

"The weekly tips give me the ability to engage more with customers. The more I engage, the easier it becomes to provide the outstanding service each customer deserves."

—**Trever,** *Customer Service Representative*

Why Rapport Matters

Customer service is inherently about interactions between humans.

Mediocre customer service is transactional. People might be friendly and courteous, but that's about as far as it goes. The average service experience doesn't leave customers feeling special or remembering the person who served them.

> *Great customer service almost*
> *always includes a memorable*
> *person who made you feel great.*

Think of your favorite place to be a customer. It could be a local restaurant, your favorite coffee shop, your barber or hair stylist, or even a tire shop. Wherever it is, your interactions with the people who work there help make the experience special.

It's human nature for us to enjoy an experience more when we like the people involved. Customers become more forgiving of mistakes. They empathize with us when we struggle to solve a problem for them. Customers who like us actively root for us to succeed and become more likely to do their part to make the service interaction positive.

The tips in this chapter focus on ways you can build rapport with your customers.

Some tips work best when you can spend a little time with the people you serve, while others can be applied even if you have just a few seconds. Many can be adapted to use via multiple customer service channels, such as phone, email, or chat.

TIP #2

Be You

You work with customers because you're good with people and have a great personality, right?

Resist the temptation to let your personality get buried beneath bad policies, challenging customers, or demanding bosses. Instead, put your personal stamp on the service you provide.

Here are a few questions to help you release your personality at work:

- What do you have in common with your customers that could serve as a conversation starter?

- Can you become an expert in some aspect of your company that would make you a "go-to" person for that area?

- What are you known for amongst your friends? Can you bring some of that to work?

There's one caveat: while customer interactions are increasingly informal, we must **still be professional**. So make sure you stay true to yourself, but make sure you're also staying professional with the people you serve!

TIP #3

Serve One Customer at a Time

A colleague of mine once said, "You can only serve one customer at a time."

Those words have stayed with me. There are times when we get busy, but each customer deserves our full focus and attention. "Busy" is never a valid excuse for poor service.

Here are some examples of how to stay focused on the *one customer* you're serving:

- Smile and make eye contact, even when you feel the pressure of a long line.

- Keep in mind this is probably the first time the person is asking this question, even if you've answered the same question from a thousand other customers.

- Block out distractions and listen intently. You never know when you'll uncover an opportunity to deliver outstanding service!

There are three clear benefits to giving each customer the attention they deserve.

First, that customer will be happier with the service they receive.

Second, you're more likely to satisfy all their needs when you give them your full attention—and that means fewer repeat contacts.

And finally, customers often become more patient about waiting when they see you give exceptional service to someone else.

TIP #4

Make the
First Move

When I was in high school, I worked as a retail sales associate in a clothing store. This experience taught me the importance of making the first move when helping customers. I also learned that *how* I made my first move was almost as important as making it.

POOR EXAMPLE

Wait for customers to come to you. Your customers know where to find you, so they can contact you if they have any questions. Some of my co-workers in the clothing store took this approach. Sales would generally go down when they were on duty.

GOOD EXAMPLE

Be proactive. Initiate contact with your customers and ask, "May I help you?" I generally got good reactions when I did this at the clothing store, although I also noticed very few people actually took me up on the offer.

GREAT EXAMPLE

Customers often don't know what type of questions they have or what help they might need. You can overcome this by **initiating the conversation**.

When I worked in retail, I learned to ask customers what brought them into the store today. That often sparked a conversation about what they were looking for and made it easy for me to find ways to help them.

Use Positive Body Language and Tone

Have you ever heard a customer service rep say, *"I'm sorry,"* but you felt they weren't sorry at all? This could be because their body language and tone didn't convey the same message as their words. You can use body language and tone to convey a more positive message when serving a customer in person or over the phone.

BODY LANGUAGE

Positive body language makes you appear more friendly and puts your customer at ease. Here are a few body language tips.

- **Smile.** Some of us don't smile naturally, so work on developing the habit.

- Avoid crossing your arms, stuffing your hands in your pockets, or other body positions that make you appear closed off and unapproachable.

- Stand up (or sit up) straight. This makes you look more friendly and also gives your voice a more pleasant, confident tone.

TONE

Speak to your customers in a warm, pleasant tone. This will make it easier for them to relate to you and feel the sincerity behind your words. Your tone will often adjust itself naturally if you follow the body language tips listed above. For example, your tone will automatically become more **warm and pleasant** if you smile and sit up straight, as if the person were directly in front of you and not on the phone.

TIP #6

Learn and Use Customer Names

Dale Carnegie once remarked that the sweetest sound to a person is the sound of their own name. Calling customers by name is a great way to establish rapport.

Here are a few general tips for learning a customer's name:

- Ask your customer directly

- Get their name from paperwork, such as an invoice or work order

- If you're a cashier, you can get their name from a credit card or identification

- Hotel associates often capture names from luggage tags or valet tickets

The big question:
Should you call customers by their first or last name?

In most situations, first names are perfectly acceptable and increasingly preferred by customers. However, it's important to keep in mind the Platinum Rule: **Treat customers the way they want to be treated.** When in doubt, use their last name or ask which they prefer.

Another trick is to introduce yourself and ask for their name. If they just give their first name, you can call them by their first name. If they give their first and last name, call them by their last name until they invite you to use their first name.

TIP #7

Make Sure Customers Know Your Name

You can personalize your service if you learn and use customer names. But did you know that customers tend to give even higher ratings when they know *your* name?

A review of customer satisfaction surveys reveals that customers who mentioned an employee by name are two to three times more likely to give the **highest rating.**

Here are a few tips to ensure customers know your name:

- Introduce yourself

- Invite customers to ask for you personally if they need assistance

- Hand customers a business card with your name on it

- Write your name on a receipt

- Use their name in conversation (it encourages them to remember yours)

Remember that we all tend to forget names quickly without a little repetition. Find a way to remind your customer of your name a couple of times so it will stick with them.

The Five Question Technique

Anyone can start a conversation with a customer using the Five Question Technique! Here's how it works:

STEP 1: Think of five questions you might use to initiate a conversation with a customer about themselves or their needs. Here are some examples:

- A waiter might ask,
  "Have you dined with us before?"

- A technical support agent might ask,
  "How is everything else working?"

- A retail associate might ask,
  "Are you looking for something in particular?"

- A hotel associate might ask,
  "How is your stay so far?"

- A parking lot attendant might ask,
  "Do you work here or are you just visiting today?"

STEP 2: Use one of your five questions to engage a customer in a conversation whenever it's appropriate.

That's it! The key to this technique is having the questions prepared ahead of time so you're always ready for a little small talk that might lead to big service.

TIP #9

Check Your Email Before Sending It

Customer service emails are frequently misunderstood, misconstrued, or simply miss the mark. Here's a quick checklist you can use to review your emails before sending them. You won't use this for every email, but try using it with a few until it becomes a habit.

- **TONE:** Will the tone of the email sound friendly to someone who doesn't know you?

- **READABILITY:** Does the email include appropriate grammar, punctuation, and spelling?

- **ACTION-ORIENTED:** Did you get to the main point in the first paragraph?

- **HELPFULNESS:** Does it provide additional information the recipient is likely to need?

- **IMAGE:** Is the email professionally written?

Some organizations have a brand style guide that can help you write customer emails that **reflect your company's brand voice.** These guides often make helpful suggestions on impactful words and phrasing. Check with your marketing department to see if your company has one.

TIP #10

Use "We," Not "They"

Try to use the word "**we**" instead of "they" when referring to your company with a customer.

Why? Your customer naturally thinks of you and your company as one and the same. Customer service representatives tend to use the word "they" when dealing with something negative, but this can make your customer think you aren't committed to the job.

Here are a few examples:

- "They typically take two days to get that done" becomes **"We typically get that done in two days."**

- "They won't let me do that for you" becomes **"Here's what we are able to do."**

- "They will be with you in just a minute" becomes **"We will be with you in just a minute."**

TIP[#]11

Friendly Follow-Up

Customers sometimes mention something off-hand that you can use later to build rapport. For example, someone might mention they're about to go on vacation. Using the "friendly follow-up," you could ask about their vacation the next time you see them.

This shows the customer you're paying attention and makes them feel valued.

It can be difficult to keep track of these little details about each customer, especially if you serve a lot of people. Fortunately, most customer relationship management systems have a feature that allows you to write notes or set reminders to follow up with someone.

TIP #12

Build an Interest List

How well do you know your customers on a personal level?

For example, I know that one of my clients is obsessed with CrossFit. Another client is a huge fan of 80s and 90s heavy metal. Still another client is an avid outdoor enthusiast who enjoys hiking and camping.

This information helps build rapport. Learning a little about your customers' interests, their families, and other things that are important to them allows you to demonstrate genuine caring on a personal level.

You can track this information by building what I call an **interest list**. It's really just a collection of notes about your customers beyond the normal name, email address, and phone number in your contact database.

Access your interest list when
communicating with a customer and
use it to ask about something you
know your customer cares about.

TIP #13

Find Something in Common

Customer service professionals who excel at building rap-port with their customers are masters at finding something they have in common with each person they serve. **Common ground** allows us to break the ice and talk about something we both care about.

Here are a few examples:

- A physical therapist put their patient at ease by discussing their mutual love of the same professional basketball team.

- A hair stylist made a new client feel more welcome by chatting about their mutual enthusiasm for wine.

- A call center representative empathized with customers who were victims of a hurricane by sharing his own experiences helping family members recover from a flood.

Of course, to find something in common, you have to **pay attention and ask questions**. Even when finding common ground isn't easy, paying attention and asking questions are two skills that never go out of style!

TIP #14

Give Preferential Treatment

Repeat customers like to be **acknowledged**. One way to do this is by learning their preferences and incorporating them into your service.

For example, I often eat breakfast at a local diner. Kathy, one of the servers, typically asks me, "Do you need to see a menu today or will you have the usual?" It makes me feel valued to know Kathy remembers my order, but I also appreciate her asking just in case.

*What do you know about your repeat customers that you can use to provide **even better** service?*

TIP #15

Answer the
Phone with
Enthusiasm

We create a first impression every time we answer the phone, but that doesn't mean we always put our best foot forward.

The phone can feel like an interruption for those of us who handle calls infrequently. This can make it difficult to focus our attention on the caller the moment we answer and give our greeting.

People who spend most of their time on the phone face the different challenge of handling so many calls it becomes tiring. This can make it difficult to give the last caller of the day the same level of positive energy that the first caller received.

Try to give a warm and pleasant
greeting each and every time
you answer the phone.

Some contact center agents put a small mirror near the phone to remind themselves to smile and use **positive body language**. Another technique is to imagine you're greeting a person who's right in front of you.

TIP #16

Use the 10 and 5 Rule

The 10 and 5 Rule is famous in the hospitality industry as a simple reminder to consistently greet people that you encounter.

10 FEET: Give customers a non-verbal greeting, such as a smile or wave, when they're 10 feet away from you.

5 FEET: Greet customers verbally when they're 5 feet away from you.

Why is the 10 and 5 Rule important and effective? Because it reminds you to walk with your head up while looking for opportunities to serve. It creates a **customer service zone** around you that makes you more approachable and may lead you to discover an unexpected service opportunity.

You can modify the 10 and 5 Rule to suit your needs. For example, I like to use a 20 and 10 Rule so I greet even more people.

TIP #17

Take a Break and Recharge

Building rapport with customers can be difficult when you're tired.

Unfortunately, the fast-paced nature of many customer service jobs wears us out. Continuously jumping from one task to another can lead to something called **Directed Attention Fatigue.** Here are some of the symptoms:

- Distractibility

- Irritability

- Impatience

- Indecisiveness

- Difficulty starting or finishing tasks

Do any of these apply to you? Many customer service employees go on break and continue to multitask. They get out their phones and text, chat, surf the web, check social media, and play games. All of this can make Directed Attention Fatigue even worse.

The only way to recover is to rest. Try taking a **real break**. Unplug. Read a book or listen to music.

Take a walk outside if it's a nice day.

Let your brain stop spinning for just a moment and you'll feel better.

TIP #18

Focus on Lifetime Value

Chris Zane, founder of Zane's Cycles, made his company famous for customer service by focusing on each customer's **Lifetime Value.** He calculated that customers spent an average of $12,500 at his store over their lifetime. Keeping this impressive number in mind made it easier for employees to focus on building a long-term relationship with every customer rather than viewing each sale as merely a single transaction.

Companies that lose sight of Lifetime Value often nickel and dime customers. For example, a local frozen yogurt shop stopped giving out free taster samples because management worried that customers would abuse the privilege. What they overlooked is that many frequent customers like to try out new flavors on each visit. Eliminating free samples made going to the yogurt shop less fun, which cost the store business.

You can focus on lifetime value by asking two simple questions.

- How much will your average customer spend with you over their lifetime?

- What would you be willing to do to create, strengthen, and preserve that relationship?

You can learn more by checking out Chris Zane's excellent book on customer service, *Reinventing the Wheel.*

BONUS TIP

Be Helpful

One of the best ways to create **rapport** with your customers is to be helpful.

My wife and I once checked into a small inn. We were immediately blown away by the helpfulness of the associate who assisted us.

She asked if we had made dinner plans. When we said we had not, she recommended a local restaurant within walking distance and even called to make us a reservation. Later, when we were leaving to walk to the restaurant, she handed us a pair of flashlights since the short stroll to the restaurant took us along a dark road.

Everything about this person seemed focused on helping us enjoy our stay.

She was friendly, asked about our needs, and cheerfully made suggestions. It was her obvious desire to help that made her **instantly likable!**

CHAPTER FOUR: EXCEED EXPECTATIONS

"Excellent customer service begins with me, and Jeff's Tip of the Week gives me that power. Smiling while on the phone lets the customer know that I care and am happy to assist."

—**Laura,** *Tech Help*

The Truth About Exceeding Expectations

Many customer service experts champion the idea of making every customer say *"Wow!"* It sounds great in theory, but it's just not realistic.

Every customer is different. What might wow one customer could leave the next one unimpressed. It can also be costly and time-consuming to try to wow every customer, every time.

People can also be fickle. What wows a customer one time will soon become the expectation, which means you need to raise the bar higher and higher if you want to continue to impress customers in the same way.

The good news is that you can create memorable customer service without setting off in an unrealistic quest to deliver a wow in every single interaction. Shep Hyken outlined a very good, practical definition of amazing customer service in his book, *The Amazement Revolution*:

"Amazing customer service is a consistently and predictably better-than-average customer experience."

In an era of rampant service failures and nasty customer ser-vice surprises, being consistently good will stand out in your customers' minds. We can exceed expectations over the long run by delivering quality service our customers can count on.

There are two ways to deliver consistently good service.

First, we give ourselves a chance to be consistently good in our customers' eyes if we can **meet or slightly exceed their expectations**. To do that, we need to listen carefully to our customers so we can understand exactly what their needs and expectations are.

The second thing we can do is **seize the occasional opportunity for greatness**. There are definitely times when a wow experience is called for. The challenge for many customer service professionals lies in recognizing the opportunity and being ready to take the right action in the moment.

The following tips focus on both understanding your customers and seizing those occasional opportunities to go beyond the call of duty.

TIP #19

Customers Determine the Extra Mile

Your level of effort does not necessarily match the quality of service you provide. That's because your customer, not you, decides whether your service is poor, good, or outstanding.

Sometimes you'll give every ounce of effort you have and employ every customer service technique you know, but the customer will still be unhappy. Other times, you'll barely lift a finger, and your customer will be ecstatic.

That's because outstanding customer service is defined as service that **exceeds the expectations of the customer**. The challenge is that every customer has slightly different expectations!

Here's a simple way to ensure you are truly going the extra mile:

1. Learn your customer's individual expectations

2. Find ways to exceed those expectations

3. Repeat

Never assume that something you
do will delight your customer.

Pay careful attention to how your customers react and adjust accordingly!

TIP #20

Win the Moments of Truth

Providing outstanding service that exceeds customers' expectations requires us to win the moments of truth.

What is a moment of truth? It's **a situation that represents a crossroads in the customer's experience.** Go the wrong way, and the customer will have a very unpleasant memory. Go the right way, and you may earn a customer for life.

Here is an example of a moment of truth that earned American Airlines my loyalty for many years:

....

I was checking in for my flight home after a long business trip when I learned that the flight had been cancelled due to bad weather. There wasn't another flight out until the next morning.

The ticketing agent told me that the airline wasn't required to provide hotel accommodations for passengers if the cancellation was weather related. However, he also told me that weather wasn't yet officially listed in his computer system as the reason for cancellation. He decided to bend the rules and handed me a voucher for a nice hotel that night.

I wasn't getting home, but at least I had a comfortable place to stay!

....

Think about the moments of truth your customers encounter when you serve them. Pay careful attention to your customers' needs during these moments, and you'll be more likely to create an impression of outstanding service.

TIP #21

Avoid Multitasking

Nearly every customer service job description lists "multitasking" as a required skill. Did you know that multitasking hurts customer service?

That's because humans can only process **one conscious thought at a time**. We work slower and make more mistakes when we try to do multiple things at once that require our full attention.

Here are some common examples of multitasking that can lead to **service failures:**

- Typing an email while speaking to another customer

- Talking to a co-worker while serving a customer

- Responding to a text while having a conversation

The scary part about multitasking is how constant busyness can convince us we're being more productive, rather than the opposite: working inefficiently.

A great way to experience how multitasking can hurt performance is to try a Stroop Test. Give it a try and see how you do: **http://faculty.washington.edu/chudler/java/ready.html**

TIP #22

Cut Afternoon Caffeine

The afternoon comes and you're dragging. Naturally, you turn to a cup of coffee, a soda, or some other caffeine source for a quick pick-me-up.

That pick-me-up helps you concentrate on serving your customers better. But it also sets off a chain reaction that ultimately makes it harder to focus.

That's because caffeine takes about 24 hours to work its way out of your system.

Your afternoon caffeine is still buzzing in your veins when you try to sleep that night. Your sleep quality declines as a result, which leads to more fatigue the next day.

That leads to, you guessed it, that familiar sluggish feeling the next afternoon.

Skip the caffeine next time you feel tired in the afternoon. Try some light exercise instead, perhaps coupled with a healthy snack. Bake that into your routine for a few days and you might be surprised at how much **more energy** you have!

TIP #23

Paraphrase
to Confirm
Understanding

Misunderstandings can and will occur in customer service. We think we heard one thing, but our customer actually said something else. Even if you heard what the customer said, that may not be exactly what they meant!

A misunderstanding may start small, but it could lead to wasted time, frustration, or even a lost customer.

A good way to avoid miscommunication is to confirm your understanding by paraphrasing. Here's how:

1. Listen carefully to your customer.

2. Provide a short summary of what you just heard.

3. Ask your customer if you got it right.

TIP #24

Slow Down When Reading Email

Email can be very convenient, but it can also make it difficult to understand what a customer really wants without a lot of back and forth.

Years ago, I managed a team that served customers via email. One of my roles as the manager was to periodically review my agents' emails for quality and coach them on opportunities for improvement. When I first started reviewing emails, I quickly noticed that more than 30 percent of the emails my team was writing missed something important from the customer's message.

How could this happen?!

Sometimes my agents were in a hurry and read the customer's email too quickly. Other times, the customer wasn't very clear and their message was difficult to decipher.

Here are two very simple tips to avoid misunderstanding a customer's needs via email.

TIP #1: Before responding, take a deep breath, slow down, and ask, "What do they really want?"

TIP #2: If it takes more than two emails to figure out a customer's needs, pick up the phone and call.

TIP #25

Avoid
Assumptions

We stop listening as soon as we start assuming. It's easy to assume you know what a customer is asking for if you've encountered a similar situation many times in the past. The danger is that your customer may want something just a little different.

You can avoid assumptions by **listening intently** and trying to understand what each individual customer needs. This can be difficult, because the brain tends to stop listening as soon as we think we know what the other person is going to say!

> *It requires effort and practice to maintain your focus on listening and avoid making assumptions.*

Once you know what they need, you can find ways to exceed their expectations.

TIP #26

Anticipate the Next Question

It's good to avoid assumptions when listening to a customer talk. When serving a customer via a written channel such as email, chat, or social media, it's often smart to do the opposite!

A great way to provide outstanding service via email is to make some assumptions about what the customer needs so you can anticipate the next question and answer that one, too.

For example, a customer might email technical support to ask for help setting up the voice mail on her new office phone system. A good customer service professional would reply quickly with the answer.

> *A great customer service professional would reply quickly with the answer **and** would try to anticipate additional questions.*

For instance, the customer could also need help setting up an out-of-office message, so the rep could include a link to step-by-step instructions on how to do that. This avoids additional emails and makes it easier for the customer.

TIP #27

Listen for Emotional Needs

Customers often have underlying emotional needs that must be met for them to feel like they've received extraordinary service.

For example, a customer might describe a problem they've had with your product or service. A good customer service rep will try to fix the problem. **An outstanding customer service rep** will understand that the customer also has an emotional need to be acknowledged for the time they've wasted and the disappointment of experiencing the problem.

The next time you serve a customer, particularly some-one who's experiencing a problem, see if you can uncover an emotional need. Be careful—customers rarely tell you about these needs directly. You'll need a strong **sense of empathy** to discover them!

TIP #28

Set Appropriate Expectations

Customers judge our service by how well the experience aligns with their expectations. Sometimes we can influence a customer's expectations so we are better able to meet them.

· ·

Example:

Let's say a customer asks you to do something that takes 30 minutes for you to do. You probably tell your customer you'll get it done in 30 minutes, right?

· ·

That's a very dangerous promise. What if something unexpected comes up and it takes you longer than 30 minutes to complete? That could be a service failure in the eyes of the customer, because you've taken longer than you promised.

A better approach is to set expectations that provide you with some wiggle room while still being acceptable to your customer.

If the task will take you 30 minutes, why not see if the customer will agree to a one-hour turnaround time? Getting back to the customer within 30 minutes will exceed their expectations. If something comes up and it takes you an hour, you've simply met your customer's expectations and nobody is upset.

TIP #29

Use the Platinum Rule

Gold used to be the king of precious metals, and *The Golden Rule* of customer service was a popular reminder. "Treat customers the way you'd want to be treated," seemed like great advice.

Today, platinum has taken the top spot on the list of coveted metals, and *The Platinum Rule* has replaced the golden rule as sage customer service advice.

PLATINUM RULE: Treat customers the way **they** want to be treated.

The key to applying the platinum rule is to avoid making assumptions about how a customer likes to be served. Find out what's **most important** to each individual and then strive to deliver that service.

TIP #30

Treat Everyone Like a VIP

You can make every customer feel like they are getting the VIP treatment by tactfully pointing out something you are doing just for them.

Here's an example:

. . . .

I was on a business trip and checked into the hotel after a long day of travel. Chris, the front desk associate, welcomed me with a warm smile and proceeded to check me in. He appeared to be looking at several room choices on his computer while he said to me, "I want to make sure we put you in a really good room."

After a few seconds he said, "Here's a good one!" and finished the check-in process.

. . . .

When I got to the room I was blown away. It was a very nice two-room suite! Now, that's VIP treatment.

Later, I learned that all the hotel's rooms were two-room suites—but I didn't care because Chris had **made me feel great**.

A few months later, I returned to the hotel on another trip. Chris was working behind the counter again, and I got in his line even though the line for another associate was shorter. Chris went through the same routine of trying to find a great room just for me. I was on to him this time, but I didn't mind. I still felt like a VIP.

TIP #31

Make Directions Easy

Many of us have to give driving directions to a customer or show customers how to walk to a particular place within our store, restaurant, or hotel. Here are two great ways to do that.

DRIVING DIRECTIONS:

Verbal directions can get confusing after three steps, so offer your customers a map or a set of written directions instead. This is helpful even if you have to draw a map or write down the turns on a piece of paper. Make sure you provide visual cues to help your customers know they're on track, such as, **"You'll see a gas station on the right. That's Ash Street—turn right there."**

WALKING DIRECTIONS:

Whenever possible, walk your customer to their destination yourself so they won't get lost and so you can offer extra assistance. If you can't do this, give them clear, concise directions and visual cues just like you would if they were driving.

Write it down if it takes more than three steps, or your customer will get confused!

TIP #32

Add Some Extra Shine!

I learned this tip from one of my clients, Ideal Plumbing, Heating, Air, and Electrical. (The company has a terrific web address: **idealservice.com**.)

Ideal's plumbers, electricians, HVAC technicians, and other workers use a very effective customer service technique. They always take care to clean up the area surrounding their repair work so it has a little extra shine.

This small step creates a positive impression for three reasons.

First, home repairs are often messy, so this extra service saves their customers some effort.

Second, home repairs can be very stressful for the homeowner, so putting some extra shine on the repair helps the customer quickly feel better.

And finally, cleaning up the area spotlights the technician's high standard of workmanship, giving the customer confidence that the repair was done correctly.

Not all of us regularly clean up messes as a part of our job, but there are ways we can put some extra shine on the work we do. Find that opportunity and you'll stand out, too!

TIP #33

Do an After Action Review on Great Service

We tend to review the situation when things go wrong, but how about when things go right? The "after action review" is a great technique to use when your customers are elated so you can figure out how to do it more often.

Here's how it works:

STEP 1: Identify situations where customers are obviously very happy with the service they've received.

STEP 2: Determine what you did to contribute to the customer's outstanding experience. (You may also want to take note of any factors that were beyond your direct control, such as a special sale or that the customer was in a great mood to begin with.)

STEP 3: Decide what you will do to get a similar result the next time you serve a customer in the same situation. The idea is to deliberately repeat what's working rather than leave it to chance.

TIP #34

Send Handwritten Notes

Handwritten notes can make a **huge impression!**

Customers appreciate a written thank you for their business. It's personal, and the sender obviously put a bit of thought into it. Most of us default to the convenience of an email or a form letter, but there are a few simple steps you can take to make note writing almost as easy.

1. **Keep a box of note cards handy.** This way, you can write the note as soon as something good happens.

2. **Be brief but descriptive.** A good note is only a few sentences long. Just make sure you use those few sentences to describe why you appreciate your customer.

3. Deliver the letter as soon as you can. **Speed is good.**

I send out at least one handwritten note per week. I've often seen them on a client's desk weeks later. I bet my competitor's email was simply read and filed...or discarded!

TIP #35

Be Careful
with Extras

We're taught to always go the extra mile. You can't go wrong with giving a customer a little extra, right?

Well, sometimes you can.

A free dessert at a restaurant can backfire if the guests are already stuffed or watching their diet. Do they eat something they don't want or reject the gift?

An upgrade to the deluxe package at the car wash can backfire if the customer is in a hurry or is sickened by the smell of air freshener.

Upgrading an airline passenger's seat to an exit row can backfire if it separates them from the rest of their family.

Try to see things through your customer's eyes before giving your customer anything extra.

And when in doubt, ask. It shows you care, and it might help avoid an uncomfortable situation.

BONUS TIP

Find Your Lagniappe

Marketing expert Stan Phelps wrote about the concept of lagniappe in his book, *The Purple Goldfish.*

Technically, "lagniappe" is a small gift given to a customer at the time of purchase. Phelps broadens this to mean an "unexpected surprise that's thrown in for good measure to achieve product differentiation, drive retention, and promote word of mouth."

Here are just a few examples:

- Customers at Jason's Deli can always treat themselves to free ice cream.

- Any part under $1 is given away for free at Zane's Cycles.

- When you buy a suit at Men's Warehouse, you can get it pressed for free—forever.

I had to think long and hard about this one since I'm a consultant. My eventual solution? All my clients get ongoing email and phone support, even after the consulting assignment ends. They can still email or call me for advice or assistance at no additional charge. This doesn't take a lot of time and I enjoy staying up-to-date with my clients to hear about their successes.

So, what low cost and simple lagniappes will **delight** your customers?

CHAPTER FIVE: SOLVE PROBLEMS

"The tips I use the most are:
Avoid Trigger Words, Use 'We' not 'They,'
Find Something in Common, Take a
Break and Recharge!, and Tell the Truth.

All of the tips have had an awesome impact
on getting customers to open up and
know that they are being listened to."

—Alexis, *Brand Ambassador*

Why Solving Problems Is So Critical

Solving problems is an essential part of good customer service. But have you ever considered why?

It turns out there are two big reasons.

The first is that negative experiences tend to be much more memorable than positive ones. And customers are more likely to complain about poor service than share a compliment about good service.

The second reason is that we tend to remember situations during which we experienced a **significant emotional shift**. A customer who experiences a successful resolution to a problem may experience relief, gratitude, and happiness. That's a big shift from the frustration, anxiety, and anger the customer probably felt when first encountering the issue.

Customer service professionals make an incredible difference in the lives of the people they serve when they effectively and consistently solve problems.

It's not always easy, so here are some tips that can make it a little easier.

NOTES

TIP #36

Expand Your Influence

Some customers are extremely difficult to work with. They routinely leave you frustrated, frazzled, and flummoxed despite your best efforts to please them.

You have two options the next time you encounter this type of person:

OPTION #1: Handle things exactly the same way. (Prepare to be frustrated once again.)

OPTION #2: Expand your influence and try to get a better result.

Here's how the "expand your influence" concept works:

1. Draw a circle on a piece of paper.

2. Outside the circle, write down things you can't control, such as what happened to your customer before your interaction, how your customer treated you, or even what your customer had for breakfast. (Angry Man Cereal, perhaps?)

3. Inside the circle, write down things you can directly control, such as how you respond to a difficult customer or what you do to help them feel better.

The goal is to find a way to expand your influence in these difficult situations. You can do this in two ways.

First, **stop worrying about the things you can't control**. (Easier said than done, I know!)

Second, add to the list of things you can control. Experiment with changing your own behavior, and see if you get a better result.

TIP #37

Stop
Complaining

We've all been tempted to complain about a difficult customer. Perhaps they were unreasonable, a bit light on brains, or just plain mean.

Let's say you encounter a grumpy customer who just won't be satisfied. Afterwards, you complain about it to a coworker. This conversation makes you feel better, because it validates how smart you are, how dumb the customer was, and the unfairness of it all.

Unfortunately, that conversation will stick with you the next time you work with a similar customer, and you'll be unlikely to get a better result.

Here's another approach to the same situation.

Let's say you encounter a grumpy customer who just can't be satisfied. Afterwards, you tell a coworker about how frustrated you were by the situation. Together, you confirm that you did a good job, *and* you also brainstorm a few ways you might get better results in the future.

> *Then the next time you work with*
> *a similar customer, you'll get a*
> *better result because of having*
> *learned from the last experience.*

TIP #**38**

Empathize with Customers

Many customer service issues can be solved quickly and with little or no cost by simply expressing empathy.

The challenge is that empathy requires two things from customer service providers.

First, we must have a relatable experience similar to what our customer is going through. Second, we must have the presence of mind to **demonstrate** that we acknowledge and understand how our customer is feeling.

Here are a few ways you can express empathy:

- Tell the customer directly that you know how it feels to be in their situation.

- Make an empathetic statement such as, "I can understand why you'd be frustrated."

- Pay careful attention to your tone of voice. A warm and soothing tone conveys empathy, but a short, monotone delivery can signal that you don't care.

Remember, the purpose of using empathy is to **make your customer feel acknowledged and valuable**. Avoid shifting the focus from them to you by telling them your story (unless they ask) or suggesting in any way that you're worse off than they are.

TIP #39

Take It
Personally

You often hear that the key to helping an angry and upset customer is to avoid taking it personally.

I couldn't disagree more!

The more personally you take the problem, the more likely you are to help.

Imagine you encounter an angry customer. If you refuse to take it personally, you might come across as an uncaring, policy-enforcing robot.

Take it personally, however, and you start handling the situation as though the customer is a **good friend in need**. You see through their anger because you know they aren't really angry at you, and you empathize with their situation.

The empathy you feel for the customer inspires you to go the extra mile to find solutions. Your genuine desire to make it happen prompts you to check back with the customer until the problem is resolved and they are happy once again.

TIP #40

Tell the Truth

It may be tempting to exaggerate or bend the facts a little to make a customer feel better about a problem. Unfortunately, this tactic often makes things worse in the long run when the customer discovers you gave them inaccurate information.

A better way to handle difficult situations is to tell customers the truth. And then tell them what you plan to do about it.

Here's an example:

My colleague, George, once had to tell 800 airline passengers that their flights were cancelled due to an ice storm. It was a Sunday and flights weren't scheduled to resume until Wednesday.

George knew the **only option** was to tell the truth, even though people would be upset with the news. He stood in front of the crowd, announced the flight delay, and then explained his plan to get everyone re-accommodated as quickly as possible.

Passengers weren't thrilled, but at least they now had the information they needed to make informed decisions about their travel.

TIP #41

Bend the Rules

The greatest customer service lessons come from customers themselves. One of my favorites is a customer who said to me, **"Sometimes you have to bend a few rules to make it happen."**

So true!

I had just given him a laundry list of reasons why I couldn't get his order produced and shipped by the time he wanted it. He and I both knew it was a one-day job that was going to take two weeks because of my company's rigid policies and inefficient processes. My customer's comment stopped me in my tracks and made me realize I didn't add any value to the relationship if I couldn't help my customer achieve his goals.

Needless to say, I bent a few rules to make sure the customer was happy and didn't take his business elsewhere.

It's a good lesson for us all:
bend (but don't break) the rules when
necessary to do the right thing and
retain your customer's business.

TIP #42

Be the Point Person

It's amazing how many customer service problems occur because everyone assumes everyone else is doing their job correctly. If I take a call from a customer who really needs some information from my co-worker Mary, I might be tempted to assume my work is done once I give Mary the message, "John Jones called with a question for you."

This works if Mary calls Mr. Jones back right away and provides the answer. But what if she doesn't call? Mr. Jones spoke with me, not Mary, so it would be my fault. Or worse, he'll blame all of us.

A better approach that **prevents problems** is to accept responsibility and be the "point person" for your customer. This can work in a number of ways, all of them resulting in you ensuring that the customer is taken care of.

EXAMPLE 1: Get the answer from Mary and call the customer back yourself.

EXAMPLE 2: Do a warm hand-off. This involves making sure Mary knows you've passed the customer along to her and the customer knows Mary will be responding to his question.

TIP #43

The Pre-Emptive Acknowledgement

The pre-emptive acknowledgement is the customer service professional's secret weapon against negative emotions. It's very simple to understand, but spotting situations where you can use it effectively can take a little practice. Here's how it works:

- **STEP 1:** Spot a problem before the customer points it out.

The key here is to spot the problem before the customer has a chance to complain. (Once the customer gets angry, you've lost your chance to use the pre-emptive acknowledgement.) For example, you might notice a customer who's been waiting in line or on hold.

- **STEP 2:** Acknowledge the situation before the customer complains.

You can do this by apologizing, demonstrating empathy, or thanking the customer for their patience. Your acknowledgement must **preempt the customer's complaint or anger** for this technique to work. If you acknowledge the situation first, the customer is likely to be okay (as long as you handle it). If you wait for the customer to get upset, your job will be much harder.

- **STEP 3:** Redirect the interaction to focus on a solution rather than the problem.

For example: *"I'm sorry about the wait, and thank you for being so patient! Let's get you taken care of!"*

TIP #44

Acknowledge and Refocus

Taking ownership is sometimes confused with accepting blame, but it's really about accepting *responsibility* for solving a problem. A great way to take ownership (and defuse any anger) is through the Acknowledge and Refocus technique.

1. Acknowledge the problem or service failure.

This conveys empathy and helps the customer feel heard and valued.

2. Refocus on a solution.

Being solution-oriented prevents you from getting stuck on discussing blame and will give your customer confidence that **you're here to help**.

TIP #45

Avoid Trigger Words

There are certain words that, when used in the wrong place at the wrong time, can set off a customer's anger. These are called "trigger words." They often make customers angry, because they communicate a lack of caring or—even worse—they make the customer feel powerless.

You can avoid unnecessarily aggravating customers in tense situations by replacing trigger words with words or phrases that are **less confrontational and more empowering**.

Here are some examples:

- Replace "No" by finding a way to say "**Yes.**" If that's not possible, at least try to give your customer some options.

- Replace "You have to" with an invitation or a request such as, "**Let's try**" or "Will you please?"

- Replace "Can't" with "**Can**" by focusing on what's possible.

TIP #46

Avoid Quoting Policy

Customers often bristle at the word "policy," because it's usually used to tell them they can't do something they want to do. Artful customer service reps sidestep potential anger by helping customers understand the benefits.

Here are a few options you can choose rather than stating "It's our policy":

SAFETY. Some policies are designed with safety in mind. Explain to your customer that you want them to be safe.

EFFICIENCY. Policies are sometimes put in place so you can service customers more efficiently. Tell your customer how they'll receive better service by doing it your way.

FAIRNESS. A few policies are put in place to make things fair for all customers. If this is the case, try to help your customer understand the bigger picture.

TIP #47

Overcorrect Problems

There's a great line in the book *Human Sigma*, by John H. Fleming and Jim Asplund: ***"Feelings are facts."***

Customers use feelings to form their perception about the service they receive. These feelings are much stronger and more important than what actually happened.

Service failures can create strong feelings about poor service. Research shows that fixing the problem might not be enough to make the customer feel good again.

If we want our customer to feel great, we have to overcorrect.

Here are some examples:

- A winery shipped wine to the wrong address. They fixed the problem by sending a new shipment to the correct address and overcorrected by letting the first recipient keep the wine they incorrectly received.

- A cable repair technician fixed a glitch in the customer's cable system and then overcorrected by showing the customer how to boost their Wi-Fi reception.

- A technical support agent helped a customer access a locked account and then overcorrected by showing the customer some new features that would save time.

In each of these cases, the customer went from feeling bad about the problem to feeling great about the extra level of service they received. All because of the overcorrect.

The Partner Technique

You'll have better luck serving angry customers if you make them feel like you're on their side. This is called the Partner Technique.

Here are some examples of using partner behaviors:

- Shift your body language so you're standing side-by-side to face the problem together.

- Listen carefully to customers so they feel heard.

- Use collaborative words like "**We**" and "**Let's.**"

It's hard to be upset at someone who wants to help. Most customers naturally calm down when they realize you're listening to their issue and trying to be helpful.

ONE FINAL NOTE: Being on the customer's side doesn't mean you aren't on your company's side. It just means you're making an effort to understand your customer and help them succeed.

TIP #49

The Good Cop, Bad Cop Technique

When a customer's frustration connects you to the problem, it doesn't matter whether or not you caused it. The customer can't get over their anger as long as they are interacting with you.

One way to overcome this issue is the good cop, bad cop technique. The customer is angry at you, which makes you the bad cop in this situation. All you have to do is introduce a coworker or a supervisor who can be the good cop and take over the interaction.

I've seen this get great results time and time again.

> *A new person on the scene*
> *instantly helps the customer calm*
> *down and accept assistance.*

This is a tough technique for some people, because they confuse being the bad cop with being bad at service. This isn't true at all. Using the good cop, bad cop technique takes an **advanced professional who's able to put their own ego aside** to help a customer feel better, even if it means getting someone else involved.

TIP #50

Share Customer Feedback

When you interact with a lot of customers, you hear plenty of stories—good, bad, and sometimes ugly.

What you may not realize is that this means a lot of **valuable** customer feedback comes to you. This is insight you can use to improve your company's products and services.

Here are some things you can do with customer feedback:

- Keep track of common complaints and share them with your boss, the product development team, and anyone else who can make a difference.

- Pass compliments along to your coworkers so they know they've made an impact.

- Encourage customers to complete customer satisfaction surveys.

TIP #51

Beware of Icebergs

It's tempting to write off service failures as one-time problems, especially if you found a way to make that customer happy again.

What if it wasn't a one-time problem, but the result of a flaw in your service delivery system? In that case, the problem is likely to be repeated many more times, and many more customers will become angry before it gets solved.

Customer service professionals should always be wary of "icebergs." An iceberg is a seemingly small problem that is actually a big, mean problem hiding under the surface.

Here are some simple questions to help you check for icebergs when you encounter a service problem:

- Might the same problem exist in other places?

- What caused the problem?

- Who else is affected?

TIP #52

Anchor Your Attitude

An attitude anchor is a great way to keep our own negative feelings neutralized, especially when dealing with an upset or difficult customer.

The concept works by focusing on something positive that "anchors" your attitude where it needs to be to deliver outstanding service.

You can use attitude anchors to maintain a positive attitude or to help recover your positive attitude after a difficult interaction.

Attitude anchors vary from person to person, but here are a few examples:

- Pictures of family or friends

- Inspirational or funny quotes

- Upbeat music

- Conversation with family or friends

- Humor, including jokes and cartoons

- Going for a walk

Even Free Ice Cream Can Make People Angry

One of the most difficult aspects of customer service is the fact that **you cannot make every customer happy.**

Ben & Jerry's holds an annual free ice cream day where the chain gives away free ice cream to customers. This is a great promotion that regularly delights over a million fans.

Incredibly, I've witnessed customers who found a way to be angry about free ice cream day. They complained about the line, the ice cream selection, or even the size of the servings. How someone can get upset about free ice cream is beyond me, yet it happens.

It just goes to show that no matter how many customers you please, there will always be one customer who finds a way to be unhappy. The challenge lies in not letting that one customer get you down.

Don't give up!

Keep trying to make as many customers as possible happy and **feel good** about all the customers you're able to serve.

CHAPTER SIX: RESOURCES FOR CUSTOMER SERVICE LEADERS

"My team and I center our weekly meetings around the Customer Service Tip of the Week. *We discuss the tip and look at current customers and conversations that we're having and how we can apply Jeff's advice."*

—**Nicholas Gaston,** *Head of Customer Support, Proposify*

Many people who subscribe to the weekly *Customer Service Tip of the Week* emails are customer service leaders like Nicholas. They subscribe to get ideas for training topics, use the tips to lead discussions in team meetings, and forward the tips to employees with their own message attached.

That's why I've written this chapter specifically for customer service leaders, providing activities you can use to **keep your team focused on customer service.**

The chapter is divided into four sections so you can quickly skim and scan to find the right idea for the right situation:

SECTION 1: Create a weekly plan

SECTION 2: Coach employees to improve their skills

SECTION 3: Five ways to use the tips with your team

SECTION 4: Additional resources to keep learning

. . . .

Section 1: Create a Weekly Plan

One of the challenges of leading employees is getting everyone to focus on the same thing. You have to repeat your message over and over before people truly absorb it and understand its importance. At the same time, you run the risk of having employees tune you out if you repeat the same message too often or never vary your delivery.

It's a delicate balance!

That's where the weekly plan comes in.

It works by setting a customer service theme for a period of time, such as a month, quarter, or even a year, and then identifying a specific tip for the team to work on each week during the period. I recommend picking a monthly topic, since most businesses already do a lot of business planning around the monthly cycle, though you can select whatever timeframe works best for your team.

Here's how it works:

STEP 1: Review the team's performance.

Gather the data you use to evaluate service quality in your organization. This could be customer service survey results, trend reports on the top complaints, quality monitoring, secret shopper results, or anything else you use to evaluate your success.

STEP 2: Use the performance data from Step 1 to select the upcoming month's focus area (assuming you're working on a monthly schedule).

For example, let's say you notice a lot of complaints about abrupt or rude employees. You might make "building rapport" your theme to help employees focus on creating a warm and friendly impression with the people they serve.

STEP 3: Call a meeting to discuss the theme and select one theme-related tip for each week of the month.

One way to do this is to have each person on the team read through this book and select their top three or four tips. For instance, if your theme for the month is building rapport, you can have the team read through the building rapport tips in Chapter Three. You can then see which tips get the most votes to finalize the ones you'll focus on during the month.

STEP 4: At the start of each week, remind your team which tip was selected for that week.

You can do this in a team meeting, via email, a note on a bulletin board, or even discuss it in one-on-one conversations. Research shows we get our message across more effectively when we use multiple communication channels, so it never hurts to remind people about the current week's tip using several methods.

STEP 5: Collect stories and feedback at the end of the week to highlight how people used the tip and what happened as a result.

You can use this opportunity to share the next week's tip, too.

STEP 6: Evaluate your progress at the end of the month and share your results with the team.

Here are a few discussion questions to guide you:

- Did the team improve performance?

- What success stories can you share?

- Are there some continued challenges?

Repeat the exercise to select a new theme for the next month (or quarter, year, etc.), asking your team to identify a new set of customer service tips to focus on. This helps establish a routine around continuous improvement while always focusing on a fresh topic so the process doesn't become stale.

. . . .

Section 2: Coaching Individual Employees

Customer service leaders spend a lot of time coaching employees to help them improve their performance. The *Customer Service Tip of the Week* can be an excellent resource guide to help you identify specific tips and suggestions to help employees improve.

STEP 1: Select a challenge or topic.

Start by identifying a specific challenge you want your employee to work on. Perhaps it's listening skills, working with upset customers, or using questions to better identify customer needs.

STEP 2: Use the "tips by challenge" list in Chapter One to find relevant tips.

You can use this list to find specific ideas for whatever you're working on with your employee. Pick one or two that are most relevant to the situation.

STEP 3: Discuss the challenge and the tips with your employee.

Meet with them to discuss the challenge. Share the tips you selected as a suggested approach to improving performance.

STEP 4: Get your employee's commitment to try using the tips.

You can even share this book with your employee and see what ideas they have. There might be different tips they would rather try that could also be effective. Ask your employee to describe how they plan to use the tips, and set a date when you'll meet again to discuss progress.

STEP 5: Follow up with your employee to evaluate how their performance has changed since the coaching discussion.

Be sure to recognize them for making an effort to improve, especially if they've made some progress on the issue you were coaching them on!

. . . .

Section 3: Five Ways to Use These Tips with Your Team

Customer service leaders often share how they use the Customer *Service Tip of the Week* emails with their teams. Here are five of their suggestions that you can implement using tips from this book.

SUGGESTION #1: Set weekly meeting topics.

Many customer service teams have a standing weekly meeting to discuss positive trends, review customer complaints, and find ways to continue improving service. Select a tip to discuss in each meeting and challenge your employees to practice using it for the next week. Follow up with everyone at the next meeting and ask them to share success stories or obstacles they encountered.

SUGGESTION #2: Forward a tip with your suggestions.

You have my permission to copy the tips from this book and forward them to your team. (The only thing I ask in return is that you clearly identify this book as the source, and only use them internally.) Many customer service leaders add their own suggestions to the tips to make them more specific and relevant to their company or the team. You could also invite employees to reply to the email with their ideas for using the tip with customers.

SUGGESTION #3: Use the tips for your newsletter or bulletin board.

Some teams have a newsletter, bulletin board, or other publication where they share customer service news and tips. You may use the tips from this book in your internal publication to share them with your team. (Just like suggestion #2, my request is that you please cite this book as the source of the tip.)

SUGGESTION #4: Create training based on the tips.

Customer service leaders often schedule training sessions to help keep their employees' skills sharp. You can draw on these tips to find training topics for your next class. Once again, you may freely copy the tips for internal use (provided you cite this book as the source).

SUGGESTION #5: Reinforce other training programs.

The *Customer Service Tip of the Week* was originally created when a client asked for a resource to help her reinforce some of the topics we'd covered in a workshop. This is a great way to use these tips! Select a few that connect with a recent training program, and forward the tips at regular intervals to help keep your employees' skills fresh.

. . . .

Section 4: Additional Resources

A single resource alone is rarely enough. Whether it's a book, a training class, or an email newsletter, a message grows stale if it's repeated over and over again in the same way. That's why it's a good idea to use a variety of resources to continue developing your team.

Here are a few resources that can help you keep your employees focused on outstanding customer service.

WEEKLY EMAILS

You can enroll yourself and your team to receive weekly customer service reminders via email. You'll receive one email with a tip each week when you register for the *Customer Service Tip of the Week*. Sign up here: **https://www.toistersolutions. com/tips**

TRAINING VIDEOS

I have quite a few training videos on LinkedIn Learning and Lynda.com. These platforms also contain excellent training programs from such notable customer service experts as Brad Cleveland and Leslie O'Flahavan.

Here are just a few topics:

- Customer Service Foundations

- Phone-Based Customer Service

- Working with Upset Customers

- Innovative Customer Service Techniques

- Managing a Customer Service Team

I know many readers already have either a LinkedIn Premium or a Lynda.com account, which means you already have access to this content!

- LinkedIn Premium: **https://premium.linkedin.com**

- LinkedIn Learning: **https://www.linkedin.com/learning/ instructors/jeff-toister**

- Lynda.com: **https://www.lynda.com/JeffToister**

Both platforms have a 30-day trial option available. The trial account gives you access to the entire training library, which covers an enormous range of topics that go beyond customer service to leadership, marketing, and even graphic design.

BOOKS

The *Customer Service Tip of the Week* is intended to be a tactical guide to improving customer service. If you're looking for a more strategic view, try my previous book, *The Service Culture Handbook: A Step-by-Step Guide to Getting Your Employees Obsessed with Customer Service*. The book is available on Amazon and other online retailers. You can learn more and read a sample chapter on the book's website: **https://www. serviceculturebook.com**

Here's a selection of books from other authors that are tremendously informative and useful for frontline employees. All of them can be found on Amazon.

- *Be Your Customer's Hero,* by Adam Toporek

- *Be Amazing or Go Home,* by Shep Hyken

- *Kaleidoscope,* by Chip Bell

BLOGS

There are a number of terrific blogs that can help you stay up-to-date on the latest customer service news and trends. Of course, I highly recommend my own *Inside Customer Service* blog, which you can find at **https://www.toistersolutions. com/blog**.

Here are other blogs I regularly read and enjoy:

- *Customer Service Life:* **http://customerservicelife.com**

- *Shep Hyken's Customer Service Blog:* **https://hyken.com/blog**

- *Help Scout Customer Loyalty Blog:* **https://www.helpscout.net/blog**

PODCASTS

Podcasts are a great way to increase your knowledge or just get focused while you're commuting to and from work. Here are a few of my favorites:

- *CallTalk:* **http://resources.benchmarkportal.com/calltalk**

- *The Net Promoter System:* **http://www. netpromotersystem.com/resources/podcast.aspx**

- *Crack the Customer Code:* **http://crackthecustomercode.com**

- *Frank Reactions:* **https://frankonlinemarketing.com/show**

- *Navigating the Customer Experience:* **http://yaniquegrant.com/portfolio-item/ navigating-customer-experience-podcast**

ME!

I'm happy to be a resource for you. Please contact me if you have a question about a specific tip, a success story to share, or if you encounter an obstacle along the way.

EMAIL: jeff@toistersolutions.com

CALL/TEXT: 619-955-7946

Getting your team excited about customer service and keeping them focused is not an easy task. It takes a strong commitment, hard work, and a lot of patience. It's my hope that the resources you find in *Customer Service Tip of the Week* will help you continue your journey to building and sustaining a strong service culture within your organization!

Made in the USA
Middletown, DE
13 December 2018